IKOJO

IHEANYI ANUNUSO

HANYVISION

UNITED KINGDOM/UNITED STATES/ NIGERIA

Copyright © 2024 By Iheanyi Anunuso

All Rights Reserved.

ISBN - 978-1-7397772-5-8

CHAPTER ONE

I still remember the drive to my mum's ancestral village in Ife, Ezinihitte Mbaise in Imo State, from our home in Owerri, the state capital, where we resided back in the 1980's and 90's on the temporary campus of the Federal University of Technology, Owerri.

Sitting, or for a more factual description, squeezing into the back seat of the Peugeot 504 that my father drove and maintained pristinely, with the rest of my 5 siblings, as he drove the one-hour journey to see our maternal grandmother, waiting in that rather majestic home my grandfather had built as a doctor in his later years, but didn't get to live in very long, as he passed away when I was five...

As a child, those journeys were always memorable, not just because it was yet another chance of going on the road and seeing the sights of the land, or the chance to see our grandmom and consume the inevitable feast she would put out for the endless appetites of her grandchildren. But, especially for me, to hold on to the headrests of the driver's seat where my father sat (yes, we didn't use, or care for seatbelts at the back of the car, or were there even any? Can't honestly remember) and encourage him to overtake as many cars as possible, was the best of times.

He honestly did not really need any of my encouragement, as he was an expert, fast driver himself who delighted in overtaking slower cars on the road, the way his oldest son, and former overtake instigator, drives now.

The end of the journey was always the same no matter the route with which you approached the house, as there were several depending on road and weather conditions. The seemingly endless sight of palm trees in the horizon, slowly giving way to the edifice built in the mid-1970s, a few years after the end of the Biafra War.

That edifice was not just a personal, if not unlikely achievement for the late Dr David Ikojo, but was a microcosm of the reemergence of the Igbo people from underneath the carnage that was the end of the Civil War in 1970. My maternal grandfather, having survived not just living close to the warfront for virtually all of the war, had also abandoned his medical career in the United Kingdom in 1967 to get back home, along with Grandma Malinda Ikojo, to my then teenage mum, Catherine.

I'm obviously not here writing today without their exceptional sacrifice.

With Grandad David gone to be with our ancestors, Grandma Malinda kept the legacy of the family going in that great house. We would undertake the journey regularly, at least once a month, alternating with going to the ancestral town of my father, Atta, in Ikeduru L.G.A, which we'll get to later.

Sometimes, the visit to my maternal village would be a single day one, where we would go early and return the same day, but at other times, usually during holiday periods we would sleep over for a few days or more.

On such occasions, we would experience all the trappings of village life, having adventures all around Ofeama, the village in Ife that my mother was from, a vast land that ran along the side of the Imo River, the massive river that the state got its name from, and which served as the border between the Mbaise and Ngwa people, two of the biggest sub nations in all of Igbo land.

I loved going down to the river, walking down the steep descent into the valley that the river flowed through. In later visits, when I was old enough to come on my own, I would go down to the river just an hour after dawn every morning to enjoy the peaceful silence of the early morning hours.

At other times in the early days, we were privileged to be around when the elders of the Ikojo clan would hold their meetings. As a kid, I knew them all, as the first thing my Mum and Grandma would do after we arrived and had eaten whatever meal had been prepared, would be to take us round to each of the houses of each member of the Ikojo clan, and beyond, where would spend time greeting everyone, from the town famous hunter Dee Ezeonye, to the Anglican Reverend, Uncle Peter, to Dee Kaku, who after a while had trouble seeing us, as his sight deteriorated with age…

Being present for meetings, organized either by our parents for their friends or neighbors, or as was the case in the villages, Clan, or Kindred gatherings, put together to discuss salient issues of the day, was always a joy for us children. Not because of the potential topics of discussion, most of which we didn't understand at the time, but rather, the food that was usually prepared for such occasions.

As we would come to understand and appreciate later in life, food cooked over fire and charcoal, would always taste better than food cooked on gas, never mind in a microwave! Due to the number of people expected for such events, food tended to be cooked in big pots and on open fires by the women of the house, with us the kids helping as much as we could under supervision. We looked forward to "party rice," pepper soup and ugba when the cooking was done, our "reward" for having to hang around for the meeting…

I however, being the oldest and having some responsibilities in helping make sure that my younger siblings were kept somewhat in check whilst the meeting was held, always managed to hang around the meeting, listening to as much of the meetings as my attention span could hold, which was unusual for my age, but I had grown up as an intellectually curious child, picking up and studying books of the history of Egyptian, Greek and Roman mythology by the time I was seven or eight years old. Maybe that early display of intellectualism was a byproduct of having a Professor of Industrial Chemistry for a father, and a pioneer journalist in the state for a mother, who always brought back newspapers from work, that I was only too happy go through quickly and neatly, before my Dad was ready to go through them…

On this occasion of the Kindred meeting, my normally curious self, had a keen ear open as I listened to a sudden argument that emanated from one of the elders at the meeting.

"No. There was never an E as a part of the letters in the name." argued an elder in the shadow of the night. "It has always been I-K-O-J-O. No other letters have ever been a part of it."

"But it means nothing in Igbo language." Replied another elder. "That's why we thought that maybe, there was a letter missing, which would make it have more meaning."

"I.K.E.O.J.O. would make more sense in Igbo language, even if not in a good way" Replied the first elder smiling, "But that has never been the spelling of the name at any time of our history."

"I wonder where the name came from?" A lady asked. "I once heard it was a name in Ghana, but I'm not sure…"

My curiosity was at a hundred percent, as I listened to the rest of the arguments over my mother's family name and would remember that meeting for the rest of my life.

Unlike a lot of Igbo families with old names, that might be considered "not virtuous" by the Christian religion which came into our land in its present/more modern form some 200 years earlier, and were encouraged to change such names to "more acceptable ones", my maternal clan refused and kept the name in the form that they had always known it as.

I am eternally proud of that decision, as it is rare position to stand on, and even more especially, as they are the only Igbo family to hold that name.

I never forgot the meeting of that night, and my youthful curiosity blossomed into a wholehearted adult search for the origins of the name that baffled many that had come before me.

That search, would take me to the other side of the home continent, to an amazing region and people so far away from mine, and hitherto, seemingly no connection or official acknowledgement between the two…

CHAPTER TWO

The flight from Brussels to Entebbe International airport in Uganda via Brussels Air, was a long one. It started from Heathrow Airport in London, where I lived, on a short connecting flight to the main journey.

The nearly 12-hour journey included a stopover in Kigali, Rwanda to drop off passengers, before continuing to its East African neighbor to the north. There wasn't much to see from the plane at that time of the night, so I made a promise to myself that I would one day return to see the Rwandan capital, and the rest of country that had made a spectacular recovery, both physically and culturally, just under thirty years after the tragic ethnic clashes of 1994…

We finally landed at Entebbe at about midnight, and after clearing customs, I sought a means of transportation that would take me to the guesthouse that I had booked a couple of days earlier.

I had never been to Uganda previously, or any other country in East Africa. Neither did I know anyone from the country. As my taxi drove me from the airport along unfamiliar roads and neighborhoods, I felt a broad smile break out on my face in the darkness as I realized that I had finally made the leap of fate on the first leg of a journey, and to ask a question that had intrigued me since I was a boy.

After what seemed like an age on the road, in the dark of night with virtually no other cars present on either side of the road, we arrived at my destination, The Blue Monkey Guesthouse, which was tucked away in a quiet neighborhood in Entebbe.

I was welcomed inside and to my room by a man who I would come to know as one half of the German couple who owned the place. The place looked clean and beautifully decorated inside. The outsides, I would come to admire in the morning, but for now, all I wanted was a shower, a bed, and of course, the Wi-Fi password!

As I lay in bed at 2am in the morning, tired from my travels, exhilarated at the thought of what was to come, but which I hadn't planned as it was a step into the unknown, I thought back to the circumstances that had brought me to Uganda, in my quest to discover an answer to that decades-long mystery… Where does the name Ikojo, come from?

*

For years, and long after I had grown too old to be the cheerleader of my father's overtakes from the back of the car and instead, was the one doing the driving when we went home to visit my maternal grandmother, the thought of the family name would come into my mind, generally with the pride of being a part of the only family in an ethnic group of tens of millions that had that name, but at other times hoping to unlock the mystery of the name's origins.

I always kept an eye, and an ear, open for any occurrences of the name that I came across, either in print or being called. But alas, no joy. Every time I saw or heard the name, they were inevitably related to the great family of Mbaise, whether I knew them or not.

But the world is never still. Each year, decade and century bring forth, political changes, innovation and refinement of the industrial complex that dictate the rise and fall of great nations and economies.

As the nineties gave way to the 2000's, so did methods of communication and study evolve. Phones became smaller and then cheaper, enabling easier communication between people wherever they might be. At the same time the internet replaced libraries as the chief arbiter of information for researchers and the curious, with its endless resource of easily accessible knowledge.

This hotbed of easily accessible knowledge would in turn give a platform for social media networks, which enabled people to keep tabs on each other wherever they might be in the world, as well as share and critique knowledge of all kinds, leading to enhanced communication between people, whether they be friends or not, succeeding in pulling people of the world from faraway lands and cultures into something of a global village.

This phenomena of easily accessible phones and knowledge, and of course, I finally deciding to get a smartphone, having never been one to join trends just for the sake of joining, would eventually lead me to finding the answers to the long-held questions I had about the origins of my maternal ancestral family name.

One day, for no reason, just on a whim, I decided to type the name Ikojo into the google search engine and look through the results. There wasn't any urgency or flash of inspiration that encouraged me on this occasion. I had done this previously and only seen the names of my cousins and other family members, with notable social media presence or information posts. Nothing extra that I hadn't seen or known before, or at least, nothing containing any knowledge that I needed or cared about.

On this occasion however, a new entry popped up as I scrolled down, or at least one that I hadn't seen before.

The entry unveiled a social media account belonging to a John Bosco Ikojo…in Uganda!

In my mind, I had always thought that quest to find the origins of the name Ikojo, whilst obviously not in South-Eastern Nigeria, the home of Igbo land, might be found in any of the hundreds of ethnic groups located in Nigeria, the most ethnically diverse country in the world. Or maybe, if outside Nigeria, might be found with one of the many ethnic groups that resided within the West African sub-continent. Never had I ever thought, not even in my most wildly imaginative explorer dreams, would I have thought that a potential answer to my queries would reside in a completely different part of Africa, some 2300 miles or 3700 km away!

Quickly, I started to browse through all I could find on the man from Uganda. His social media footprint didn't reveal much, but as I perused through the other information that I could find out about him, I discovered that he was a politician and a Member of Parliament in Uganda.

I looked at the region that he represented, the place where he was from, and discovered he was from a place called Bukedea. A quick search of the area didn't produce much to catch my eye, outside of posts from the proud inhabitants of the area describing its beauty and traditions.

Deciding to expand my knowledge of the area, I searched to find the language of the people of Bukedea and their origins.

The chronicle of the origins of people of that region, they were called the Teso people whose population spread across Eastern Uganda and Western Kenya, showed their journey from the old country of Kemet, the land that is now called Egypt, and through Ethiopia to their present location in Eastern Uganda and neighboring Kenya.

The story of their origins brought a smile to my face, as I was already well immersed into the story of the origins of many of the ethnic groups of Africa, and wasn't at all surprised with the links to the world's oldest civilization, something it had in common with some of the ethnic groups spread through the great continent, including mine, the Igbo, which we will get into later…

That feeling of familiarity with the origin story, along with the need to find out why my mother's family name would be appearing in the faraway lands of Eastern Africa, prompted me to search for the phrase "Igbo and Iteso" Iteso being the name given to an individual member of the Teso ethnic group.

The results of that search, as it revealed itself across my screen, would immediately prompt me to plan and arrange for a trip to the Pearl of Africa, as Uganda is nicknamed, with the confidence that after years of fruitless search and speculation, I was finally on the right track…

CHAPTER THREE

I woke up the following morning, well rested and very hungry. I had recently developed a distaste for airplane food, and its aftereffects on me…even the aroma of the food as the trolleys moved up and down the aisles, had begun to make my stomach churn.

This development put me off from having food on flights, and as you can imagine, being on a twelve-hour flight to Entebbe left me famished. Pre-planning made me bring a packet of peanuts on the flight, but as I stretchered on the bed that morning, my stomach started making noises to alert me of its disenchantment with the situation…

The time on my phone as I reached across the bed showed it as a few minutes past 7am, it was my 7am alarm that had woken me, so I hopped out of my bed and went to my window to catch my first sight of Uganda in the daytime.

There was a lady hanging wet clothes on the line as I pulled back the curtains, and I quickly closed the curtains as I realized I wasn't quite dressed. I made my way to the bathroom with toothbrush and paste in hand to take a shower, so I could go out to the guest areas after and find out what I could get for breakfast.

Albrecht, one half of the German couple who was kind enough to wait up for me to arrive in the wee hours of the morning, had given me brief direction of what was available at the Guesthouse after daybreak.

As I got to the living room area, I met Anna, the Ugandan lady I had seen hanging clothes on the line outside earlier, who now guided me through the options available for the complimentary free breakfast package.

The options were European, so I ordered for the option with sausages, baked beans and orange juice and went out to the front porch to see what the outside spaces looked like.

The view was magnificent!

In the distance, you could see planes descending towards the airport, flying above the never-ending watery expanse that was Lake Victoria…

Andrea, Albrecht's wife, then came over to introduce herself, as well as another guest, Karen, who had also arrived that morning.

I told her it was my first time in Uganda and how much I was looking forward to my time here, short as it was.

She and her husband had decided to retire here and build the lodge years ago and were now a fixture on the local scene.

Karen, the new visitor was also German and had been a regular visitor, having made the journey a few times now.

I informed them that I was planning to visit the Eastern region on some research I was planning to write about, and they were excited to know that I had published some books.

After spending some time talking with Karen in the garden in the morning sun when Andrea had left us to check on how things were going inside, I decided to leave the gated compound and get my first taste of the surrounding areas on my own, not least being to get close to Lake Victoria which could be seen from the elevated position of the lodge.

With some excitement in my soul, I walked along the untarred road, my eyes taking in my surroundings. Albrecht waved as he drove past me on his way back from what seemed to be a supply run for the lodge.

I made my way down towards the lake asking questions whenever I felt a bit of indecision on the way to go, even though I have a pretty good sense of direction. My people have a saying "Onye ajuju anaghi efu uzo" (They who ask questions, never get lost). I found myself walking along a much busier road with minibuses full of people on their way to the capital, Kampala.

This I knew having spoken with Anna earlier, so I could know how to get to Kampala via public transport, once I was ready to go, as my check on the route to get to Bukedea showed that I would need to go through the Ugandan capital city…

My walk of discovery now took me through what now appeared to be a busy Market area that looked very much like any local one I'd been to in Eastern Nigeria. There were provision shops, so named because they sold a bit of everything that a regular household would need on an everyday basis.

There were pharmacies selling everyday medicine, which in most rural or low-income areas which were of more use and more accessible to the local populace, taking the place of hospitals.

I saw some selling food, but not with the look of a place I'd be comfortable eating in. I grew up in Eastern Nigeria and knew how to assess eating spots wherever they might be, and whilst I was on the lookout for a place where I could try the local cuisine as the lodge wasn't serving any, I hadn't seen one that I'd be confident eating in, yet. Especially as a visitor on a first-time visit.

Finally, I arrived at the Nakiwogo Landing site with its myriad of canoes, small and medium size boats, and of course the large Ugandan government ferry that as I came to learn, conveyed people of a three-hour ride across the massive lake to Kalangala a beautiful island retreat in the middle of the world's largest freshwater lake.

A lot of people and cars were queuing to join the ferry which would begin the ride at 2pm. I looked around, hoping to see a restaurant where I could get some food, but couldn't find one.

Thinking that it was odd, I started to make my way back to the lodge after taking as many pictures of the great lake as I could, but this time deciding to keep my eyes peeled for not just food places, but any signs of hotels in the area that I might have missed on my way to the lakefront.

I'd barely walked five minutes from the lakefront, when I noticed the sign for Migingo Suites, with an arrow directing me down a side road from the main street. The quality of the sign made me know instinctively that I was headed to a good place.

I quickly made my way down the street as it wound its way down in the direction of banks of Lake Victoria, or as I prefer to call it, by its more authentic local name, Nalubaale (Mother of the Guardian gods), the name given to the lake by the Luganda people, an ancestral ethnic group in the Central Region of Uganda, and owners of the western shore of the great lake.

Little did I know that God in his infinite wisdom, had used my quest to partake in the local cuisine, to put me in the company of the one man who would the best possible guide in my quest to find the connection between my people, the Igbo people of Eastern Nigeria and the Teso people of Eastern Uganda & Western Kenya.

CHAPTER FOUR

"My name is Patrick. Nice to meet you, Iheanyi (my name is pronounced Ehane). Welcome to my hotel."

I had arrived at the gates of Migingo Suites, and after I'd gotten the attention of the security to get through, I was taken to the office of the manager, where I met Patrick Ochieng for the first time.

After I'd introduced myself, I told him of what had brought me looking for the place, to which he let out a laugh and told me to relax and not to worry about that, as he would get someone to cook me a Ugandan dish.

He then called for a lady, Marina, who as it turned out, not just was the Chief Cook for the hotel, but also was the de facto Number 2 to Mr. Ochieng and his lady. Partners in life and love.

After Marina had enquired as to my palate preferences; I didn't have any and told her I would happily take whatever she prepared, Patrick and I sat down in the office, and I began telling him of the reason I had travelled down to the Pearl of Africa.

He listened to me quietly for a minute, smiling and nodding his head as I described how I had traced the family name of my mother's family, Ikojo, to Eastern Uganda via the family name of the elected representative to the Ugandan House of Representatives, Hon. John Bosco Ikojo.

"I know him." Patrick said to my utter surprise. "My mother is from that area of Uganda, and I grew up there…"

He went on to tell me that he was a former parliament member himself, representing his constituency at the Ugandan parliament, and offered to introduce me to the Honorable member representing Bukedea, Hon. Ikojo.

That whole conversation felt surreal. I had been mentally planning my trip to go to Bukedea ever since I had made enquires of Anna over at the Blue Monkey Guesthouse, earlier. I had tried to check the logistics of making my journey by public transport across the country from Entebbe to Kampala, and then on to Bukedea.

The national train transport system wasn't functional to make that journey, at least not for travelers, so I was left with trying to plan that journey using public buses along a route I knew nothing about, to an area that I had never been to, or knew anyone that resided there.

All that mental planning still couldn't account for meeting the Honorable member representing Bukedea, the most crucial part of my entire sojourn to the Pearl of Africa.

Now, here I was talking with the owner of the hotel I had come to find food in, talking to a former legislator who was arranging to take me to the Ugandan House of Parliament to meet Hon. John Bosco Ikojo!

Marina came back in to let me know that the food had been laid out by the staff, upstairs in the dining area. Patrick asked me to go upstairs and enjoy my meal, and we could continue to talk afterwards.

I followed Marina upstairs to the balcony where I was greeted by the magnificent view of Lake Victoria flowing past just a few hundred meters away and shore on the other side, with boats and ferries making their way in either direction, as well as the occasional view of a plane landing at the Entebbe International Airport, a short distance away.

I opened the covered plates to the delightful sight of Rice and Stew along with a whole tilapia fish, thanking Marina and making sure to take a picture of my first ever Ugandan dish, before proceeding to completed devour every bit of the meal, sans bones, in the beautiful Ugandan afternoon weather, with a calm breeze emanating from the nearby lake.

Afterwards, I went back down to meet Patrick in his office where after some more discussions on my trip, I enquired about the rooms in his hotel, and after finding there was availability, made the decision to move there from the Blue Monkey as it made sense to stay at the Migongo Suites, and proceed to plan the rest of my trip from there.

It was evening when I left the hotel, exchanging greetings and saying my goodbyes with Patrick and Marina, after I'd seen the room where I'd be staying in, when I got back the next day.

As I strolled back on the road back up the road to the Blue Monkey Guesthouse, I was smiling as I wondered how my palate choices had turned my uncertain logistical plans, into a most surprising "door opening" opportunity of certainty and purpose.

The next morning after breakfast, I said my goodbyes to Andrea and Albrecht, thanking them for being such good hosts. They were happy when they knew I'd found someone to guide me on my journey east, having been aware that was where I was headed from my earlier enquires.

Karen, the German lady who was the other guest that was there, was also going to be leaving the next day, as she was engaged in philanthropic work in Uganda through her dance classes and school. She had been going to Uganda for years and could actually understand some of the culture and a language or two and made sure I was okay with where I was going, knowing it was my first time in the country. We said our goodbyes and exchanged contacts, and I told them I'd make sure they got a copy of my book when it was all done.

I then checked out, and in the cool late morning sun, strolled down the road to the bottom of the hill towards the Migingo suites, confident for the first time since I had landed in Entebbe about 48 hours earlier, as to what my plan for accomplishing my goals for the trip.

A real case of taking a forward, even if uncertain step into the unknown, in faith, and being rewarded by the reassuring feel of a foot on the rung of an ascending ladder…

CHAPTER FIVE

Patrick and I, left the hotel around 9am with the driver Moses in the SUV, having filled up the tank the previous evening in preparation for what would be a long trip.

Patrick had spoken with Hon Ikojo the previous evening to enquire as to his availability at his parliamentary office.

Based on my conversation with Patrick afterward, I got the feeling that he was as intrigued about my enquires as I had hoped he would be.

With the Honorable member's schedule now confirmed, we drove from Entebbe towards the nation's capital, Kampala, where the Parliament House was located.

On the one-hour drive along the beautifully constructed multi laned Highway that morning, I felt an excitement, as I felt that for the first time, I was on the way to unveiling a mystery that had remained unsolved for as long as time itself.

The views along the road as we drove on the partly elevated highway; it was built across some of the water that fed into the great Lake Victoria; were great and I felt like I hadn't felt in years, like the way I used to sit in the car, as my father would drive the seven-year-old me to the ancestral places. Only this time, I was on a journey to find out the hidden meaning to the most unique name of the biggest family and how it got there in the first place…

We arrived Kampala shortly after 10am, at which point Patrick messaged Hon Ikojo to see if we could proceed straight on to Parliament House.

Being a former legislator privy to the workings of parliament, Patrick asked the driver to take us to a nearby restaurant to Parliament Avenue, so we could have some food whilst waiting for a confirmation from the Honorable member.

We parked outside the Kampala Pork Planet, and went in to have some breakfast, where I ordered Pork Katogo, a delicious Ugandan delicacy of cooked green plantain (matooke) and pork emanating from the Baganda people.

Patrick ordered his meal, as did Moses while we waited. The city was bustling around us, as expected of a nation's capital. Uganda is a multi-ethnic society comprising of over 50 ethnic groups, some bigger than others. Kampala was in the Central Region, and as was the case with a lot of countries, the largest number of jobs were located there, and so drew people from all the other regions, in search of economic opportunity.

Hon Ikojo then replied to Patrick's message, he had been in an impromptu meeting debating some national policy or the other, as was to be expected of an MP.

We then made our way up the road to the parliament building a short distance away. There was a heavy military presence at the entrance, and when it got to our turn in the queue, we were asked for the reason we were there and who we came to see. They recognized Patrick, and we after a few pleasantries were exchanged, the barrier was raised, and we were directed inside.

When I think back, I'm still amazed as to the God sent gift that was Hon Patrick Ochieng. It was as if I had been granted a magic carpet ride to get to my required destinations, most of which I hadn't even planned or thought about previously. The help I received from the former Honorable member can never be overstated, and as I reminisce while writing this, it was one of the many signs I received on this trip to Uganda, which made me believe that this quest of mine, had divine guidance and Blessing. There would be more to come.

Hon Patrick being familiar with the layout of the parliament grounds, directed Moses on where to park, knowing where Hon Ikojo's office was located in the massive complex.

Moses waited near the car, finding somewhere in the complex to find shade from the emerging sun, as Patrick and I made our way to the building in search of the Honorable member representing Bukedea.

We went through security, as was mandatory, and went up the building to the floor where Hon Ikojo's office was located, knocking on the partially open door once we found the right one.

He had a visitor, a fellow legislator I believe, but once he saw Patrick, he motioned us to have a seat where the visitor seating area for his office was, whilst he concluded business with his visitor.

After a few minutes, his visitor stood up to leave and he introduced us to him, after which some pleasantries were exchanged. He motioned us to the chairs near his desk while he escorted his visitor to the door.

We waited a minute or so while I looked around the office. Neat, with a simple and functional design, where everything seemed to be arranged in good order, something I always appreciated in any environment. I've always liked a neat space…

He came back into the office, at which point Patrick introduced me as the gentleman who had come all the way from Nigeria via the UK, with some questions about the Teso people and their possible links to my people, the Igbo of South-eastern Nigeria.

I then greeted the Honorable member, introducing myself formally, before proceeding to explain the reasons why I had made the trip to the Pearl of Africa, in search of the Teso people and the people of Bukedea in particular, no thanks to my maternal lineage sharing the same surname as him.

He listened quietly, with growing fascination showing up on his face, especially as I started to describe the similarities in our languages with certain words like hands and first-born sons amongst others.

After asking a few questions about what I wanted to do with all the information that I might find out on this quest, as well as the effort to come all the way down to Uganda, he promised to help me in finding out all that I could, on this mysterious connection between our peoples and families.

He provided me with the phone numbers of two of his family members back in Bukedea, one of them older than him and the other younger, so they could assist us to meet with his kin.

We took photos commemorating the occasion, and after some ten minutes or so, catching up with Hon Patrick on the latest goings-on in politics and life, as the two had known each other for years, we said our goodbyes, thanking him for his help, and promising to keep in contact via the numbers that were exchanged.

Just like that, I had my lead through which to find information in Bukedea. I would only later realize the importance of him providing me with access to his family when we would arrive Bukedea. There is no way I would have found them on my own.

He had also asked me to meet the King of the Teso people, so that I could also get as much information as possible on the origins of the people from as official a source as was possible, checking to make sure we had the contact details of the paramount ruler of his people.

We located Moses when we got back down to the parking lot, and after Patrick exchanged greeting once again with the security at the guard outpost and caught up on any of the happenings in their lives, we proceeded on our way towards Eastern Uganda.

I could tell he, Hon Patrick Ochieng, was a very much liked politician during his time in politics, a man of the people.

The Perfect man to travel with, as I got to the conclusion of my cross-continental, culture quest…

CHAPTER SIX

We had been driving for over 2 hours before we got close to the Nile Bridge at Jinja, where we now pulled off to the side of the road for a brief stop at the Igar Plaza.

Jinja is home to the source of the longest and most famous river in Africa, the Nile, which attracts a lot of tourists. I could see tour buses rolling past with more foreigners than I'd seen in the country since I landed at the airport in Entebbe.

The Igar plaza looked well set up from the outside, and we let Moses find a parking spot he liked and join us, while we went inside to see what the place had to offer.

It was a spacious, well-planned restaurant, that like the best fast-food places that I knew in Nigeria, catered both for traditional meals, as well as popular fast-food delicacies. I saw Meat pies that looked like the ones I had grown up with back home in Nigeria, and tasted just good as I could remember, after I had purchased some.

After we had all gotten something to eat, we made our way back into the SUV, to continue on our journey. Crossing the bridge was the closest I came to seeing the source of the famous river, as we continued on to our destination towards Tororo.

Crossing the Nile Bridge at Jinja, felt like we had officially left the Central region of Uganda, and firmly now in the Eastern Region.

It was a two- and half-hour journey from Jinja to Tororo, and whilst I didn't know it at the time Patrick was already planning ahead for our meeting with the King of the Teso people.

Back in Kampala, he and Hon Ikojo and already sent messages to the King, ahead of our visit. Patrick had already thought that we wouldn't arrive at the King's home empty-handed, hence the decision to drive to Tororo, a decision he explained to me as the journey progressed.

Uganda has some of most beautiful landscape in the world in my opinion. Sometimes the vegetation doesn't look like you are in Africa, it looks like vegetation that would be found in Europe, or some other continent on the northern hemisphere. Only it isn't obviously planned like you would find in the aforementioned places, just seemed to be there naturally.

At other times, it was like I was transported back home to the other side of Africa, alternating from rich savannah, rife with rice plantations, and a full-blown tropical forest with banana and plantain farms.

One of the areas of unparalleled natural splendor on the road from Kampala to Tororo was the Mabira Forest Reserve, a vast rainforest area that is home to hundreds of species of trees, birds and butterflies that are not found anywhere else.

Just as happened later on in Jinja, we didn't stop to go to the reserve, as it wasn't our objective for the trip, which was still hours away. I would have loved to, but trees, birds and moths could wait another day. A king, especially one who was expecting us at his home, couldn't!

I didn't miss out on everything the vast reserve had to offer though, as we drove along the road, we started to see some baboons walking at the side of, and across the road.

As it turned out, these were the Olive Baboons, the stars of another reserve along the road to Tororo, the Busitema Forest Reserve. Moses stopped the car as I took pictures and a video, but learned that we were not to feed them, as per instructions from the authorities, which made sense, so as not to put the monkeys in harm's way.

After a couple of minutes, we resumed our journey to Tororo, stopping briefly so that Patrick could check on some people that he knew, as it wasn't a journey that he made frequently.

We would eventually make it to Tororo around 5pm that evening, a long cross-country journey as it was. By this time, I'd been briefed by Patrick as to what he thought to purchase to take to the King on the subsequent short(er) journey to Malaba, where we would find the King.

It had been a while since I'd gone to an African market to bargain for goods, with the added disadvantage that I didn't know the local language. So, I took Moses with me as we attempted to find a worthy bunch of plantain amongst a few other things. Patrick had gone to have his hair cut and shaped, something I didn't need to do as I had always looked after my own hair since I was in my mid-twenties.

Tororo's biggest market had been replaced by a modern indoor market which was finished only a few years earlier, but in true African style, there was still a sprawling market that existed all around it, a familiar sight to anyone used to our historical markets around Africa.

Moses and I first went into the indoor market where we purchased a few things. It felt good to once again test my skills at bargaining. The lady laughed at my attempt to bargain in the local language following Moses' lead, but she did lower are initial asking price, teaching me the correct terms of pronunciation with a laugh. I paid her original asking price anyway, as I knew this was her main source of income from experience making such transactions, back home. I had some means, and my goal was never to short hers…She still added some extras, as they always did when they appreciated your patronage, just as was done back home in Igboland.

We left the indoor market, as we realized that there were far more plantain sellers at another street, selling by the roadside. Plantain or Matooke as it's known in Uganda, features in a lot of meal choices, and so was a no-brainer to take with us as part of our gifts to the king.

Having finally picked up all the items we needed, we got back to the SUV where Patrick was waiting nearby and proceeded on the final bit of our journey that day, to see the King.

CHAPTER SEVEN

The modern palace for the King of the Iteso, Emorimor Sande Emolot, which is proposed to be built in Soroti, a city designated as the headquarters of the Iteso Kingdom, was a two- and half-hour journey northwest from Tororo. But the King, who was elected to the throne in 2022, maintained his current palace in the town of Malaba, the border town between Uganda and Kenya.

The Teso ethnic group (Iteso people simply means the people of Teso), are spread from the eastern region of Uganda and across into the western region of Kenya.

Malaba is one of the busiest crossing points between Uganda and Kenya, if not the busiest land crossing, as it sits on the highway between Kampala and Nairobi, the capital cities of Uganda and Kenya, respectively.

As we drove towards Malaba, we had started to encounter heavy traffic consisting of heavy-duty trucks, a telltale sign of the amount of goods that made its way across the two countries.

We were travelling through remote country as it was, and you could see the mountain range in the distance, and Kenya, as Patrick would inform me, was just on the other side of those mountains. However, we were getting closer to the border post, traffic had slowed to a crawl, and we were worried that we had missed a turn-off somewhere.

We pulled off to the side of the road, to an area that had a few shops and decided to ask for directions to make sure of exactly where we had missed the turn off, as Patrick was certain that we had.

This was deep in the rural areas of the country, even if google maps was able to give any type of directions, I wouldn't trust it here. This had to be done in the traditional, old-school way. Human direction. Every local would know the way to see the King…

A quick conversation between Patrick and a local gave us the answer we were looking for. We had only just missed a turn off a few mins down the road.

With all of us thanking him, we turned the SUV around, and found the right turn off from the main road, and quickly drove down the dusty rural road to the villages within.

It was getting darker now, as the time was about 6pm in the evening, and with the light fading, we kept an eye out for the road signs indicating which village we were approaching and which ones we were exiting.

We drove in this manner for about 20 mins before we decided to again pull over once we got to a certain village square and ask questions as to the King's residence.

Patrick had already been in communication with the King during the drive through the rural area, and we were expected, but there was more than one way through the area, and they couldn't be exactly sure of the one we had taken and gave us as best of a direction as they could.

Again, human direction proved helpful, and we turned back around on the lookout for markers that had been described to us.

After one final check as we passed a group of men walking along the road we were on, we found the entrance road to the King's residence, with a man from the palace waiting whom had been sent there to bring us in once we arrived.

Patrick and I alighted from the car and were directed into the King's front room by his wife the Queen, while the gifts that we brought along with us were taken round to the back for presentation later, for when the King emerged.

The King's home was well designed with a large compound, well shaded with great trees that would give great protection from the sun when needed. In the distance, just as it had been as we drove through the area, you could see the mountain range in the distance.

These, as I would come to know, were the Virunga Mountains; Mount Gahinga, Mount Muhabura, Mount Sabyinyo and of course, the largest one, Mount Elgon, an extinct volcano, were the mountains that formed the border between Uganda and Kenya, seen in the distance. I would continue to see these mountains, as my quest through the land of the Teso, progressed.

Even these incredibly impressive mountains, nor the borders between two countries, had been able to sever the links that the Teso people had kept in Western Uganda and Eastern Kenya.

The King emerged shortly after we arrived, and we rose to greet him, where I was formally introduced to him by Patrick and welcomed to the Kingdom.

After we presented the gifts that we had brought with us, and he had drinks brought forth, he then asked that I describe the quest that had brought me to distant lands.

He nodded in understanding as I described how I had discovered links, via my maternal family name, between my people, the Igbo, and his people, the Teso.

After drinks had been poured and he had enquired from Patrick as to the state of things with him, life and business, he sat back in his chair and began to talk to me on my quest, as he began to give me the history of the Teso people…

CHAPTER EIGHT
(CHAPTER IKANYKAUNI)

THE HISTORY OF THE TESO

Teso traditional story telling of their origins, state that they emigrated south from Kemet, the country the Greeks named as Egypt, the modern name that ancient country carries today.

The traditional story describes the Teso as being descendants of one of the sons of Abraham; the father of all Hebrews according to ancient scripture; Joseph, the youngest and most famous of the twelve sons of Jacob, and his marriage to a princess of Kemet (Egypt).

We do know from biblical tales in the Old Testament, that following Joseph's abandonment by his older brothers, he would eventually find favor in Ancient Egypt and rule, but I've only added this paragraph, as a bookmark and reminder that so much of the traditions, stories and beliefs transcribed in the ancient Bible, echo a lot of the traditions and culture of quite a few ethnic groups spread out through West Africa including mine, the Igbo. I will expound on a few of those later on in the book…

Going back to the story of the history of the Teso, the origin storytelling, talks of a time when the Teso people, at around the time when the Hebrew slaves had decided to leave Ancient Egypt, decided to make the journey south, following the Nile, travelling in a Southeastern route towards Abyssinia (modern day Ethiopia).

It was whilst they inhabited the mountainous area where they had temporarily settled in Abyssinia, that they became privy to the fertile lands in modern day Uganda.

The Teso were part of a larger group, and one the other ethnic groups that were a part of that movement are the Karamojong, and I bring them up as the area of Northeastern Uganda where this emigrating group settled in originally is called Karamoja.

Karamoja means "the old person is fatigued," and this town is very significant in the immigration story of this group of ancient Egyptians (people of Kemet), as it is said that it was at this point that the group began to splinter off into various groups towards the various ethnic group locations as they are today.

The town Karamoja is so named because, it was at that location that the older people of that migrating group were left at to form a community along with a few younger ones, as they could not continue on the journey to the find a permanent home.

The search for the home parallels the biblical quest of the ancient Hebrew to find the homeland promised to the descendants of Abram, as their travel path is narrated as a journey "to a land divided by small rivers originating from the Nile River, spotting the fertile area they moved to from the mountains of Abyssinia."

The name Iteso, follows the same incident at Karamoja, coined from a term when a group of young men said "ite so ibaren" meaning they were on the move to search for pasture for their livestock, after the old men of the tribe said that they could no longer travel, deciding to settle at the place they were at…

The Karamojong and Teso are a part of language group called the Eastern Nilotic people which include the Maasai of North Tanzania and Southern Kenya, the Turkana of modern-day Kenya, the Nyangatom of present-day Ethiopia, as well as the Samburu & the Toposa of South Sudan.

This geographically diverse language group that is spread across four countries in East Africa, reflect the historical path of the group's migration from the area known as modern day Egypt, through to their sojourn into modern day Ethiopia, and the final movement and dispersion through Uganda, Kenya and South Sudan.

The Teso people would settle in their present-day location of Eastern Uganda and across Mount Elgon into Western Kenya. They have historically practiced crop and animal farming, attaching great value to the land, becoming very successful at it which would eventually lead to them being targets of less successful/affluent groups in the earlier part of the 20th century.

The Iteso are very well educated, placing a premium on the acquisition of knowledge, as well as very independent minded. These attributes are similar to that of my own ethnic group all the way in Southeastern Nigeria, the Igbo.

The current generation of the Iteso is the twelfth generation of the ethnic group, with each previous generation having its distinct geographical or cultural significance; either marking a pivotal movement to their present location or have significant social interaction with another ethnic group.

The Eleventh generation is recognized as the first to interact with the Christian missionaries who brought with them Western education, and of course, conversion to Christianity.

The Twelfth and current generation is well educated, very unified and largely Christian. They still engage in animal and crop farming that have been a staple of the evolution of the Iteso culture; rice production is a very favorable business to be in due to the incredibly fertile land; but with modern day techniques that have allowed them to remain amongst the very best at it.

It was quite dark when the King and I had finished discussions on the history of the Teso people, with me taking notes and asking questions, as well as suggestions on where I could find literature on the extensive topic.

We thanked the King for allowing us in his home and for giving us his time and passing on his knowledge on the history of the Iteso. He thanked us again for the gifts that we had brought, and then rose up to escort us back outside to our vehicle.

It was about 8 pm when we made our way from Malaba to find a hotel to sleep in, as it was too late to go on to Bukedea to meet the Ikojo clan. Tororo was the closest city to Malaba, so we drove down to the city to find a suitable hotel.

After we had checked out a few, we finally decided on one close to the city center and withdrew to our rooms, to refresh and continue our journey the next day.

The restaurant service was already closed, so it was just as well that we'd had dinner at the home of the King before we left Malaba.

I was a little parched so still made my way down to the restaurant looking for a drink. Patrick had gone to check on some of his old friends in town, so it was just me basking in the glory of spending my first night in Teso country, feeling like I was home…

The elderly man at the bar, who was about closing up, let me in to choose a beverage, and I was pleasantly surprised to see a cold bottle of Krest in the fridge, a drink I hadn't seen since my secondary school days in Nigeria, back in the mid-nineties.

It felt fitting, that on a day when I was finally unravelling a thousand-year-old ancestral mystery, due to a thirst for knowledge and clarity, my actual thirst buds were being satisfied by an old favorite drink of mine, a literal blast from the past.

I thanked the elderly bartender and made my way back upstairs to my room, in anticipation of the discoveries that awaited us in Bukedea.

CHAPTER NINE

We left the hotel just after 7am, as agreed the previous night before we had headed off to our rooms. We briefly stopped at a petrol station to fill up the tank before the journey from Tororo to Bukedea.

We then proceeded in a northwesterly path along the Tororo-Mbale-Soroti Road, as we proceeded on the journey to Bukedea to find the Ikojo clan.

The journey from Tororo to Mbale, the biggest city in the Eastern Region of Uganda, and therefore one of the biggest cities with Teso speakers in all of Uganda, took just over an hour that morning, allowing me to survey the beautiful landscape that this region provided.

Tororo, apart from being the largest populated city in all of Eastern Uganda, is largest producer of cement in Uganda, with all the biggest production companies based in around the city. The reason for this became apparent as you looked around at the horizon of the city and immediately saw the large rock formation called Tororo rock, an outcrop of volcanic rock, reputed as the second largest in all of Africa and a popular tourist destination, with a trail used by visitors to get to the top.

As we drove along the road, I noticed that there were more outcrops of rock, Patrick pointing to one while saying the area had probably the largest deposit of phosphorus in Uganda and maybe Africa, with large cement producing factories around them.

Whilst we were moving away from the border between Uganda and Kenya, we were primarily heading in more or less a straight path from Tororo to Mbale, and so you could see that this was an elevated region in terms of topography even when you could no longer see the mountain range that was obvious at Malaba, the previous day.

That mountain range sprang back into magnificent view once we got to Mbale, the largest city and capital of trade in the Mbale district, as well as the second largest city in the Eastern Region of Uganda and a major hub for the Ugandan railway network in that part of the country.

The city is also reputed to be one of the early eastbound settling points for the Iteso, from whence they first made their crossing into Kenya, crossing the magnificent Mount Elgon, the crown jewel of the Virunga Mountain range, into Western Kenya.

This was the first mountain range I had ever seen in person, as I had grown up in the comparably flatter hinterlands of Eastern Nigeria, and so I was awestruck at the beauty of it and its complete domination of the landscape. This natural edifice that seemed to have been handcrafted by God himself, went on for miles, and yet again, and not for a few times on this trip to the Pearl of Africa, I was enthralled by the beauty of the landscape of the country that was Uganda.

The city of Mbale had the feel and look of a big city, as you approached and drove through it. Big commercial areas with the accompanying throng of people. We had to maneuver through early morning rush hour traffic so we could get to the Soroti Road which would get us on our way to the Bukedea District.

Whilst the city of Mbale is directly on the road between two major Teso speaking cities and districts, the major language spoken there isn't Teso, but Lugisu, a language which is mutually intelligible with the language spoken by the Luhya people of Western Kenya.

After navigating traffic through the well planned and built city, we were soon on our way to Bukedea which was only 35 kilometers or just about 40 minutes up the road.

The landscape now seemed flatter in the horizon, with rice fields began to appear, a major crop in the region, as we continued on in a northwesterly course to the home region of the Ikojo clan of Bukedea.

We passed what looked like a massive rock formation, which felt like it might have provided safe refuge to people way back in time. It was nowhere as high as the outcrop in Tororo, but rather spread itself horizontally for maybe a mile or so.

I recorded a video of it, somehow knowing as soon as I saw it as we approached, that it was special. A part of the rock formation is what you see on the cover of this work.

You could see in the distance, the mountain range that signaled the location of the Kenyan border, as we finally reached the town of Bukedea. It was a small town, with much of it built around a cluster on both sides of the road.

We hadn't had any breakfast when we left Tororo, and we decided to find a restaurant where we could get some food. We found one housed on the property of a petrol station. Patrick had been making calls to the phone numbers his Honorable colleague had provided to us in Kampala to contact his kin with, once we had arrived in Bukedea, but hadn't yet received a response.

After we'd got out of the SUV and entered the nice, neat restaurant, we found a table and checked out the menu. I never missed an opportunity to savor the local cuisine, and Patrick was helpful when I needed help with the makeup of any dishes that I wasn't sure about.

I settled on a breakfast dish called "Rolex," a unique Ugandan dish of a vegetable chapati wrapped inside a rolled egg omelet, and it was delicious.

After we'd had breakfast, one of the Kinsmen contacts provided by Hon Ikojo, Mr. Joseph Onane, returned Patrick's call, giving us directions on where to meet him in Kumi, the next town which was just twenty minutes away.

The Kumi hotel which was just a five-minute drive from the junction on the Soroti Road where Kumi, a district headquarters town, was located, was a beautifully landscaped property that immediately stood out from anything in the town. The well-designed hotel building and grounds with the well-manicured trees lined up in front, looked like it had been taken right out of a postcard.

He enquired as to whether we'd had breakfast, and after we had affirmed, and he and Patrick had exchanged pleasantries, he then asked as to the reasons for my visit to the district.

Nodding in appreciation, as I explained my cross continental cultural quest, he praised my attempt at unlocking the mystery of the family name, before picking up his phone to call his Kinsman who had been the other contact on the list provided by Hon. Ikojo.

We left after expressing our thanks for his hospitality and help in directing us to what was the crown jewel of my enquiry quest, contact with the eldest member of the Ikojo clan, the person, as he explained, who knew the history of the Ikojo clan from the beginning of time, as passed down through the generations.

As we drove back to Bukedea to meet Micheal Okwi, who was the son of the Ikojo family patriarch that we were going to meet, it dawned on me that I was about to uncover the mystery between the Ikojo family name from Igboland in Southeastern Nigeria and the one right there in the Teso speaking part of Eastern Uganda.

CHAPTER TEN
(CHAPTER IRI)
THE HISTORY OF THE IGBO PEOPLE

The Igbo people of Southeastern Nigeria (they can sometimes be referred to as "Ibo" by older publications of African cultural history) are one of the three major ethnic groups in the most populous country in all of Africa.

My people are known as the most industrious ethnic group in all of Africa, due to their propensity for business wherever they find themselves, not just in the country of Nigeria and across its borders to other countries in the West African sub region and beyond, to other countries on the home continent, but across the world in countries as far and diverse as the United States and China.

There is a long-standing joke amongst the Igbo people, that if you go anywhere in the world and can't find an Igbo man living there, you can turn around and leave the place, as there is no money to be made there.

This ability to be economically successful wherever they find themselves, and as such, dominate the commercial centers in towns and cities, has sometimes led to Igbo people being the subject of envy, and getting them caught the intricacies of religious and tribal intolerance as seen during the Presidential elections held in Nigeria in February 2023, and other times, infinitely more disastrous circumstances, as seen during the tragically brutal Civil War that raged between 1967 and 1970, called the Biafra War.

My late maternal Grandfather, Dr. David Ikojo, was living in England practicing medicine, when that war broke out, and had to hastily make his way back to the now crisis-stricken country along with my grandmother, Malinda.

They lost all they had on that journey by sea from England and the subsequent 30-month Civil War, just as so many other Igbo families did. A lot of those families lost loved ones to that war, but due to the heroism of my Grandparents and the Grace of God, they lost none of their family to the war.

Their bravery and sacrifice is the reason that I am able to author this book. It was my mum and her brother, that they abandoned everything for, to travel back and rescue. A million children were killed in the British sponsored blockade of food in that war.

Even though my mother had to live close to the various warfronts at different times during that conflict, as my Grandad was drafted as a senior officer in the medical corps for the Biafra army as soon as he arrived home, it was my mother's proximity to him, and my Grandmom who served as a field nurse; where the best available medical help was, that saved her from the fate of millions of Biafrans.

Going back to why the British government of Harold Wilson decided to be a party to such tragedy, will need for an explanation of another of the core attributes of a true Igbo man, our independence. That explanation of the core beliefs and attributes to being Igbo, essential to understanding the motivations of who we are and have always been, takes us back, way back in time…

The origins of the Igbo are varied, according to folklore, the earliest literature of Igbo culture from the first authors on Igbo history such as Olaudah Equiano, and the first observations by the British of the Igbo people from the 19th century recorded by George T. Basden, amongst others.

IGBO ORIGIN VIA FOLKLORE

Folklore traces the journey of the Igbo as starting from Kemet (Egypt), when the Hebrew tribe of Gad left Egypt due to the adverse conditions that they found themselves in during the harsh times that the Hebrew people endured in the period following the death of Joseph, in the well-known biblical story of the plight of the Hebrew at the hands of the Egyptian Pharaohs.

Gad is the seventh son of Jacob, and his lineage is traced in Genesis 46:16. This lineage trace stated in the Bible is very important, and key to the traditional origins of Igbo people, and lists the sons of Gad including, Eri, Arodi and Areli.

The oldest town in Igboland due to archaeological research is the town of Aguleri, Anambra State in Eastern Nigeria, which names Eri as its first founder and original King.

Aguleri simply means "namesake of Eri." Eri is thought to have arrived our present location in Southeastern Nigeria by travelling through Northern Africa, down through what is now Mali and then following River Niger down as it merges with River Benue, and onto the Atlantic Ocean where it empties itself.

There are other towns named "Umuleri" and "Oraeri" which mean "children of Eri" & "People of Eri" respectively. Also, if you want to talk about events that have occurred a long time in the past, you say "Erimgbe."

The Igbo just like some other African ethnic groups, use names given to children and towns as a means to preserve history, which can be seen in the previous examples.

The narration of this origin story immediately brings favorable comparisons with the ancient Hebrews of North Africa/Palestine (there was no region called the Middle East back in the day. That term is almost as new as the creation of the Suez Canal in the early 20th century.)

These ancient Hebrew attributes/characteristics that the Igbo have, will continue to come up as we use other sources of information and research to trace the history of the Igbo people.

One of those Hebrew characteristics that are unique to the Igbo people and the old Hebrew that aren't practiced by anyone else apart from the Igbo since Biblical times, was the separation of females during their menstrual period.

In Leviticus chapters 15,18 & 20, the Bible details the practice as done by the Hebrew of the Bible, where women having their periods, were moved to a house at a corner of the compound, where they were provided for and stayed until their menstrual cycle was over.

No one else in the world outside of the Igbo, observed this practice in modern times. In fact, my mother observed this practice when she was a girl in the early 1960's, confirming the truth of our people's observation of this practice.

She had to do this, as the practice no longer holds today due to the influence of Christianity in Igboland. About 99% of Igbos are Christian, following one branch of the faith or the other, which is the highest rate of any ethnic group in West Africa. I would say that the other ethnic groups in South-eastern Nigeria, neighboring the Igbo, will have close to a similar percentage. This, as the jihad that engulfed most of the northern part of West Africa, failed to enter the Southeast, as it was repeatedly beaten back by the Igbo as described in the great book (Ibos: Hebrew Exiles from Israel, Amazing Facts & Revelations by Prof. O. Alaezi)

Another ancient Hebrew practice that is performed by the Igbo from time immemorial, is the practice of circumcision done of every male child on the eighth day following birth, a practice that is followed by every Igbo, no matter where they are in the world.

Even though I was born in Leicester, England, I too was circumcised on the eighth day in accordance with the traditions of my people.

We'll now check on the descriptions of Igbo history and culture through its earliest writers.

THE FIRST MODERN DAY AUTHORS OF IGBO HISTORY

Olaudah Equiano is recognized as the first victim of the Transatlantic slave trade, to buy back his freedom around 1766, some ten years after he was captured from his Igbo village in Southeastern Nigeria.

He would move to London and join the abolitionist movement to fight against the barbaric practice and industry that captured him as an 11-year-old, transporting him across the Atlantic to the Americas.

Olaudah Equiano; who we Igbo think his real name to be Olaudah Ikwuano/Ekweonu due to the difficulty of the English language to handle the phonetics of the Igbo language, a struggle I am familiar with, as my name Iheanyi, is pronounced differently from the way it is spelt in English (pronouncing Ehane, is the closest you could correctly say it in English),would go on to publish an autobiography "The Interesting Narrative of the life of Olaudah Equiano" which would become exceptionally popular around the world, when it was released in 1789, and was heavily used as literary material in the fight against slavery long after his death, till the passing of the Slave Trade Act in Britain in 1807.

Whilst the importance and popularity of his book, was a great tool in the slavery abolitionist movement of 18th century Britain, for Igbo people, his autobiography is the oldest literary work ever written, detailing the life of the Igbo in the early 1700's.

He was captured at the age of Eleven, but as a First-born son of his family, it would appear that his father had already started to teach his young son important details about the culture of his people, something I too as a First-born son can relate to.

Olaudah was also very observant on the going's on in his community, and that trait alongside the teachings from his father, provides us with immeasurably valuable information on the life and unblemished culture of the Igbo, before they would come in contact with the colonizers.

He would also make some observations in his autobiography about the similarities he noticed between the culture of his people and the ancient Hebrews of the Bible he studied, after he had been converted to Christianity.

One of those observations was his remembrance of a Priestly clan of his people, the Igbo, who count the years, keep our calendar, and offer sacrifices and prayers on our behalf to the One True God.

This Priestly clan who helped us conduct worship, wore their beards and could only be succeeded by their sons, as the position was hereditary on the male side, a practice and exact practice of Aaron and the tribe of Levites, as detailed in the Bible in the book of Leviticus Chapter 21.

Also, they could only be buried by members of the Priestly clan, and they didn't touch the corpses of anyone else, just as in Deuteronomy Chapter 14.

It was this practice, amongst others the details of which can be found in his groundbreaking 1789 autobiography, which convinced him that his people were descended from the Hebrews of the Bible.

We are grateful for his work, as this practice is no longer in existence due to the destruction to the culture done by the advent of the Christian missionaries, whose real mission back then was to dissociate the people from their cultural practices to pave the way for acceptance of the foreigners and their subsequent colonization at the end of the 30 year Civil War fought by the British to gain access to Igboland, known as the Ekumeku Movement(1883-1914) and the Aro War(1901-1902), the only opposition encountered by the British in their quest to colonize the area known as Nigeria today.

That fierce opposition is the reason the British government have historically backed any other ethnic group, no matter how undemocratic, to rule Nigeria, as they know they will have no influence in the country's affairs, as my people are fiercely independent.

As a sidenote, in addition to being a people that worship one God, a rarity in the world from ancient times till today, just as the ancient Hebrew did, we are the world's oldest practitioners of democracy, as every town/community leader is chosen by the people, and there is no such thing as a "king of the Igbo".

All of Igboland, about a population of 40 million today, have similar culture and traditions governing them, but every town and village is independent from each other. No city/town/village can tell another what to do, an annoying trait to the British in their quest to takeover Igboland, as subduing one part, didn't ensure that the next town would give in. A fresh battle had to be fought again. This was at odds to their practice against other tribes, where all they had to target was the King, and get him to fall in line, ensuring the rest of the tribe will follow.

Also, even though Christianity would eventually become the religion of the Igbo after colonialism, the Igbo simply transferred the name of the One True God that we worshipped, Chukwu, to God of the Christian religion, as we already believed in One God, long before the Europeans.

Prof O. Alaezi's book, Ibo's: Amazing Facts & Revelations, which I've referenced previously, also goes into details about Eri's lineage, and in the tradition of Igbo culture, a lot of towns throughout the land have the names of he and he sons as part of the town name, including mine, which is Atta (from Attai) in Ikeduru L.G.A in Imo State.

It's also recorded in the aforementioned book, of the discovery by British archaeologists in 1917 of a solid bronze casting of a Star of David about 500 feet below ground. The British would also mint money for the Eastern Region using the Star of David as the main identifier in the early 1900's. See pictures towards the end of the book.

The mention of this discovery takes us to the final part of the observation of Igbo heritage and ancestry.

FIRST OBSERVATIONS OF THE BRITISH ON ARRIVAL TO IGBOLAND

As much I prefer to read literature on Igbo culture, history and ancestry written by Igbo people like

Olaudah Equiano or writers not born in Igboland but foreign born of Igbo origin like Surgeon-Major James Africanus Beale Horton (1835-1883), one of the very first Black Officer Corps of the British Army in the early 1860's, who was born in Freetown, Sierra Leone after the thwarting of the shipping of his parents to the Americas.

However, publications on Igbo culture by foreigners in the 19th century provide some insight into life and culture of the Igbo people, if you can temporarily put aside the unsavory racial terms used to describe our ancestors, for no other reason other than a false sense of superiority. Small gems of knowledge come forth, albeit unwittingly, on some of the practices of our people, like a small time-stamped window of information.

George Thomas Basden in his book "Among the Ibos of Nigeria: An Account of the Curious & Interesting Habits, Customs and Beliefs", notes that the Igbo didn't have any traditional means of making alcohol, instead relying on the natural preparation of Palm Wine, which is harvested from palm trees as is still done today, remarking that the Ibo were a sober race, playing second to no one else in terms of sobriety. However, in a sign of changing times, and a reflection of things to come, he also later noted that due to outside influences now having access to the interior of the land as colonization progressed, foreign made spirits were making their way into Igbo society, leading to hitherto unknown problems of drunkenness in the land.

But more interestingly, and more to our discussion on the origins of Igbo culture, he also noted that "certain customs rather point to Levitic influence at a more or less remote period." This statement influenced by his observation of the practice of circumcision practiced by the Igbo, as I've noted earlier in this book.

He also observed that "the Igbo language bore several interesting parallels with the Hebrew idiom."

James Africanus Beale Horton, in his book "West African Countries and Peoples (written in 1868) about the Igbo people in the aftermath of the breakthrough for the British government in following River Niger to the end of its flow into the Atlantic Ocean in 1854, noted some observations which we've noted here previously, and some others that are hitherto unknown.

Whilst remarking on the independence of each town in the land, as well as the recognition of women in Igbo society as opposed to other tribes in the region, albeit not as town/village leaders in accordance to the patriarchal ancestral lineage system of the culture(just as it was with the Hebrew of Biblical times), he recorded that the slave trade practice had died in Igboland by 1835 due to the lack of external pressure from outside groups with the abolishment of the trade in Europe, as there were no internal mechanisms amongst Igbo people to pursue the devastating human trade, even though it continued amongst other tribes in the region.

He also said that Igbos were considered the most imitative and emulative people in the whole of West Africa, "place them where you will, or introduce them to any manners or customs, you will that they very easily adapt to them. They are big-hearted, always possess a desire of superiority and make attempts to attain it or excel in what is praiseworthy, without a desire of depressing others."

Continuing on, he wrote that "the Igbo cannot be forced into anything, they become stubborn and bull-headed…As a rule, they like to see every other African, prosper…"

***

With the knowledge I had recently received from the King of the Iteso, combined with my knowledge of my people, I could already see that both tribes' ancestry could be traced to the North

Africa/Palestine area, but what I couldn't yet explain, was how my unique maternal family name from the interior areas of Southeastern Nigeria, was replicated in the interior areas of Eastern Uganda, and why.

As we pulled back into the petrol station in Bukedea, where we had just had breakfast, just over an hour ago, I couldn't wait to find my answer.

CHAPTER ELEVEN

We drove down the rural road having turned off the Mbale-Soroti Road at Bukedea, and for the second time in two days, we were driving in the same direction as elevated land springing up in the distance, and I knew we were moving east in the direction of Kenya.

Patrick and I had met up with Mike Okwi, the man Mr. Joseph Onane had called up at Kumi and directed us to meet.

After we had met up at the restaurant in Bukedea and exchanged greetings, especially between he and Patrick as they knew each other from their mutual interest and involvement in politics, we now followed him as he drove ahead of us, leading us to meet the head of the Ikojo clan.

The drive took about ten minutes, as we drove into the interior of the land of rolling hills and savannah-like vegetation.

We finally arrived at a massive compound walled round by bamboo like sticks that were each about 6 feet tall, with two medium/large sized traditionally built houses, in the middle of the compound.

Moses reversed the SUV into some shade, as Patrick and I, led by Mike, made our way to the clearing in the midst of the two houses, where a few seats had been arranged in a bit of a circle, clearly the area where visitors were received.

Dr. Akabuai Darlington, was the elder that we came to meet, and after we had been introduced to him and his sister, who came out to meet us as well, by Mike, we all made our way to the seats in the visitor area.

He was formerly one of the great African veterinarian doctors now retired and had been on missions around the continent in service of the Organization of African Unity (OAU), or the African Union (AU) as it is called today, the biggest and oldest decision-making body for all of Africa since its creation in 1963.

These trips around the African continent, allowed him to interact with many distinct cultures around the home continent, appreciating their uniqueness and diversity, as well as the various ways in which they shared similarities.

This was a part of our opening conversation after he asked for the reason that I had come from so far to meet him and his people, and I sensed that he appreciated finding a kindred spirit who was as intrigued he was in the great complexities and history of our continent.

He was the man Hon. Ikojo had wanted us to meet when we spoke in his office the previous day, and as I listened to him speak, I realized that there could have been no one better than him to teach me on the pertinent questions of my quest, than if I had made a prayer to God on the exact person to go to in all of Uganda.

Once we had gotten all opening discussions out of the way; he also asked us if we would have lunch, which we declined, citing the fact that we had some food not long ago; he sat back in his chair and proceeded to tell me the story of the Ikojo name, and how it came to be in this current location…

***

A long, long time ago, a period of great insecurity in Kemet (Egypt) caused a mass migration of the native people from the land, southwards.

There were many different ethnic groups living in Egypt at the time, and when the decision to move south was made, they decided to move in groups, probably formed according to geographical proximity of their locations in Egypt.

These groups left at different times, and in the story passed down the generations by his ancestors, Dr Akabuai names the two groups known to them on their journey south.

Note that, these are not the only groups that migrated at this time, they are just the groups that were a part of the journey that the Teso embarked on with.

The first group were called the Kalingeri group, a group that consists of the modern-day Maasai and Samburu. They are called the first group in this telling as they are recognized as the group that left, just ahead of the group Dr Akabuai's ancestors in the Teso tribe were in.

The second group, which the modern day Teso tribe were a part of in the great migration southwards, was called the Atekeri group. This group consisted of the Teso, Nyangatom and the Toposa.

Dr Akabuai's telling of his family's ancestral history, puts the location of their original home as the current location of where the Suez Canal exists today.

From there, as written here earlier, they followed the Nile, the river Omo and Lake Turkana amongst others, following and staying close to the waterways, in a southward journey through the Great Rift Valley.

At certain times during that journey, the two groups, the Kalingeri and the Atekeri, would run into one another, with the former having lingered on at a place for longer than they normally would for one reason or another.

On such occasions, both groups would team up, and working together would hunt animals for food in great and elaborately planned search parties.

The preferred animal that was hunted was the elephant, as they were plentiful and of course were a large meat source capable of feeding large groups of people. The elephant's name in the language used by both groups at the time was "Etom," a name that still exists today, as the Teso name for elephant.

There were also occasions when both groups would actually stay in a certain area long enough to engage in planting crops, but those occasions were very rare, according to Dr. Akabuai. My take on that was that this was a very long journey that took years, and to a place neither of the groups knew, and such a journey had to be fraught with uncertainty and upheaval, especially with a large group of people involved in such an undertaking.

I then asked, as to how he thought my family name had would have gotten all the way to Nigeria, some 2500 miles away, the only family that had the name and, in an area, where the name had no meaning, especially as it was more common in Uganda and Kenya, and I also finally asked him what the name meant.

He then told me something that made sense and corresponded with not just only the ancestral history of my people the Igbo, which I've written on in the previous chapter, but also of that of another West African tribe situated in Ghana, the Ewe, of travelling from what we now call Egypt, making a southwesterly journey to their current home in West Africa.

The Kalingeri and Atekeri groups were not the only groups of people to leave Egypt during that period of strife and insecurity. They were just people of a similar language pattern and strong enough cultural affinity that decided to make that journey together. They had just decided to go in what now appears to be a southeasterly direction instead, taking them to their current abodes in South Sudan, Uganda, Kenya and Tanzania.

My mum's family it appears, while clearly being of the Atekeri group due to the name they bore, had decided at some point, either prior to leaving

Egypt or after, to travel in the southwesterly direction that the other groups of people had gone, but kept their name through the length of the arduous journey and the thousands of years since arriving their present location.

With time, the original language that the family name was in was slowly forgotten, being rarely used where they were now located. But, like most great African Ethnic groups, which keep their history preserved either in stories/folk tales, the names of their cities/towns, or the names of their children and kin, my maternal family kept the original name long after its meaning was lost, an amazing feat considering the closest meaning in Igbo language could connote that it was a family name of "great evil strength."

Such names were attacked as evil by the Christian missionaries after they arrived in Igbo land in the 19th century, and a lot of Igbo families with such names are convinced to cleanse themselves of the name, to wade off evil destinies.

The Ikojo clan of Ife, Ezinihitte Mbaise, were one of the few that stubbornly refused to alter or change their exceptionally rare name, even after they changed to Christianity, even though the constantly debated where the name had come from.

It was at one of these debates, hundreds of years after the meaning of the name had been lost, that a very young me, serving refreshments at an elders meeting, had happened upon and become forever intrigued by.

Dr Akabuai went on give me the meaning of the Ikojo name, also describing the special set of circumstances that occurred for the name to be given out. We Africans tend to have circumstantial meanings to our names; either an event/occasion, a shared characteristic with someone dear in the family, whether dead or alive, and thankful prayer to our creator or a prayerful foretelling of a great destiny.

Ikojo meant "the sharp point of the arrow" and tended to be given during times of great climate change, of which the great Doctor told me have always happened over time, and in great African style, is reflected in the names given to children born at such a chaotic time.

This occasion of adverse climate conditions usually meant there was great hunger in the land as there was a famine, which made for little crop harvest and few animals.

At times like this, the newborn children were severely affected by lack of milk, which was a dietary constant in Atekeri life. When these shortages occurred, the cows were bled using the tip of the arrow, and the malnourished children then fed to keep up their protein intake.

Children born during this time, would have names that reflected the dire circumstances of that period. Ikojo, was one of the names that arose out of that circumstance.

One of the children born during such a time, might have been on that sojourn from Egypt, or in the time when the language was still viable among the family, it was the last one given, as the Ikojo name also tend also be given to greater hunters for obvious reasons, or in true African tradition, given to a child by a parent in prayerful expectation for the future.

The good doctor also smilingly told me, that he too was born during such a period in the 1940's. His name Akabuai, meant "bow."

We finished our discussions, exchanging contacts and leaving gifts in gratitude for his time, before getting into the SUV and finding our way back to the main road.

Finally, I had the answer to my decade's long curiosity, an amazing story that not just provided answers, but gave great insight into the journeys of our ancestors, the connections between our modern-day realities and our ancient history and civilization, in ways in which most modern history books couldn't or wouldn't represent.

The very notion that ancient Egyptians looked like me and my African siblings is still either a bone of contention, or outrightly scoffed at by the arrogantly minded uninformed, even though the oldest historical writings like the works of Josephus, the oldest complete work of history in living memory, published in early Roman times, confirms the fact.

For me though, it was another sign of divine favor in my quest for knowledge. Not just that I finally knew the meaning to my mum's family name, which meant "the sharp end of the arrow", but like when I found Hon Patrick Ochieng because I was looking for Ugandan local cuisine, and without whom this whole endeavor would have been almost impossible to have turned out the way it had done, that the elder that revealed it to me, Dr Akabuai, the patriarch of the Ikojo clan in Bukedea, the meaning of his name meant "bow".

The bow that released the arrow. Who would have thought…

CHAPTER TWELVE

With my sojourn to find the meaning to my maternal family name now complete, we made our way back to Entebbe.

Michael Okwi decided to travel back with us as he had business in Kampala, and so, along with another friend, we made our way back. Only this time, we used a different route from the one we had used to arrive in Bukedea. Micheal and his friend being locals, knew a quicker route.

We made our way back to Kumi, and from the junction, made a turn westwards towards the Pallisa District, driving past its beautiful land that seemed to go on forever, with vast spaces between sparsely populated areas, and filled with rice and banana plantations.

Once we got to the district headquarters situated in Pallisa, we stopped over at the office of the Resident District Commissioner Dhikusooka Majid, who welcomed us to his office, and hearing of my quest to Bukedea, called over Councilor Osako Nicholas Epaja to give me some history on the Teso people, who also were in this district. It was he that confirmed on the elite hunting prowess of the Ikojo name.

We got to Kampala about 8pm, dropping off Michael and his friend, who both had business in Kampala the next day, before continuing on to the hotel in Entebbe and arriving shortly after 9pm.

I wouldn't have much longer to spend in Uganda regrettably. Now that I was there and had found out all I had been searching for, I wanted to take my time and explore the beautiful country in its entirety.

As I lay in my bed that night, excitedly processing all the information that I uncovered earlier that day, I couldn't help but start to put together information that I had known previously with it.

The whole question of where the ancient Egyptians had disappeared to, and why they hadn't been found, became painfully obvious.

With the writings of the past 300 years by Europeans, as well as all the Hollywood films produced over the last 100 years, trying to falsely assert the ancient Egyptians were white/Caucasoid or Arab, and couldn't conceivably be of the same race/color as the rest of the people inhabiting most of the continent, for obvious reasons in the wake of the Atlantic slave trade, they had only mislead later generations on how to find them.

You see, by assuming the Ancient Egyptians were Caucasian/Arab, the world had also bought into a false narrative about the true nature of the people they were looking for.

In England, everyone speaks some variation of English or the other. Same goes for France, Spain and Portugal.

Saudi Arabia, Kuwait and Lebanon primarily speak one language, Arabic. More linguistically diversified countries in the region known today as the Middle East like Iraq and Iran might speak up to 6-10 languages. Those latter two countries however, can trace their lineage to ancient Babylon & Persia, respectively.

Hence, the false view that they were looking for a singular people or culture and language, no thanks to the stereotypes perpetuated by written and visual media over the last century, not to mention color.

The search for such a people was as much of an exercise in futility as King Saul's pursuit of David in Biblical times.

It would be like someone setting out in a few hundred years to find the Nigerian people, culture and language, after the country might have ceased to exist. There are over 250 languages and cultures in Nigeria.

A village I know in Cross River State, has spoken languages for the male and female parts of its community.

The smallest country on continental Africa is The Gambia with a population of just over 2 million people, speaks nine languages. The entire country has a land mass of just over 300 miles.

Now that we know that in actuality, it was Black Africans that lived in Ancient Egypt/Kemet, imagine how many cultures and languages that thrived across the land.

Once you can see who the ancient Egyptians truly were, you start seeing them across the continent. From the pyramids in Sudan and Southeastern Nigeria, the traits and cultural origins that tally with that of the ancient great country in Northeastern Africa.

The reasons why in Biblical times Jesus' parents and Elijah sought to evade capture in times of danger, by escaping into Egypt, now bear correlation with the ancestral stories of the Igbo and 19th century British suspicion of "Levitic influences" in Igbo culture and "Hebrew idiom" in Igbo language.

You naturally escape to areas where you would merge with the population and hide out. I, as a Black man wouldn't be escaping to Iceland or Siberia, without standing out like a sore thumb.

Also, reading through the complete works of Josephus, the man lays claim to the oldest complete work of literature in existence, you find the mention of the flight of Hebrews to Alexandria, Egypt and then on to Cyrene (Libya) in the aftermath of the Judean Wars.

Tindirma, in modern day Mali was a former Jewish settlement town that was of significance during the time of the Songhai Empire in West Africa, reflecting on the path of movement from modern day Palestine and through North Africa, the same type of paths old Igbo ancestral stories traced their journey from.

The same Umayyad and Abbasid Caliphates that would occupy Southern Europe, also ruled over Northern Africa, and their quest to Islamize the area, forced most remaining Hebrew faith settlements that wouldn't convert, to follow their kin further south into West Africa.

There have been so much disruption to the various cultures of West Africa from the Slave Trade to Colonialism, and their effect on the people, religion and the passing down of history, that I fear a lot of our history and links to a great past have been disrupted or lost.

Hopefully though, there are still stubbornly proud families, which have held onto their old names and history, leaving access to curious generations yet unborn, to follow the cultural footprints of their ancestors, and learn of the true shared history of the world's most diverse continent.

ACKNOWLEDGMENT

I would like to take the opportunity to remember my maternal grandfather, Dr. David Ikojo, who took a risk in leaving a good job in the colonial civil service of Southern Nigeria and 3 children, leaving for Ireland in the early 1950's to study for a medical degree.

He had to abandon his medical career, leaving England along with my grandmom, as the Biafra War started in 1967. He lost everything trying to get home and was given £20 at the end of the war, the price paid by the Igbo people in their fight for survival in that war.

The return to economic greatness by my people, in spite of that tremendous setback can never be spoken about enough. My Grandfather was no different. He would go on to oversee the rebuilding of all the regional hospitals in the Southeast, including the hospital now known as the Federal Medical Center in Owerri, and become the first doctor to build a private hospital in all of Mbaise.

I'm not able to write all this if he doesn't ensure that my mum was kept safe during that horrendous 30-month Civil War that claimed the lives of a million children. He would pass away from heart complications in 1982.

I also would like to thank my Grandmom, Lolo Malinda Ikojo, who will turn 94 this June, still drives her car along the roads of Mbaise and looks like she's in her 70's. She also had to work as a nurse during that war, helping my Grandad, as she also worked in that field in 1960's England after joining Grandad.

Also, while I'm here, I'd like to apologize to her for disbelieving that she had gone to the cinema to watch the "The Sound of Music" in 1965 when it was first released, because as an 8-year-old, I believed that the film had to have been shot in the 1940's during World War II…I can still remember the exasperated look on her face during those "arguments" …

A special thanks to the Hon Patrick Ochieng, Hon John Bosco Ikojo, Dr Akabuai Darlington and of course, the King of the Iteso, Emorimor Sande Emolot, without whose assistance, I would have been unable to actualize the goal of the quest that brought me to Uganda, the pearl of Africa.

Finally, to the ancestors of the Ikojo clan going back centuries. A sincere thanks on their effort to preserve their history and ancestry through time and generations born. Never allowing the turmoil of the Slave Trade, Colonialism and the institution of a new religion, as well as what other hazards they had to have faced, to deter them from leaving tributes to their footprints through time and distance, so that their children to be born would know who they were, and where they came from.

It's said that you can't know where you're going, if you don't know where you've come from…

All Thanks to God.

British Colonial Penny, with Star of David used in Igbo land in 1908.

At the Ugandan Parliament office of Hon. John Bosco Ikojo

From left to right, Hon Patrick Ochieng, me in the middle and Dr Akabuai Darlington at his home in Bukedea.

At the office of the Resident District Commissioner for Pallisa District, Dhikusooka Majid, in Pallisa.

The King of the Iteso, Emorimor Sande Emolot

My late maternal Grandfather Dr. David Ikojo, with my Grandmother Lolo Malinda Ikojo to his left and their daughter in law, Lizzy Ikojo.in the late 70's.

The late Dr. David Ikojo prescribing medication at his private hospital.

My parents, Professor Cliford Anunuso & Lady Catherine Anunuso (nee Ikojo)

Yours truly, Iheanyi Anunuso. Thanks for following me on this epic journey. God Bless.

www.ingramcontent.com/pod-product-compliance
Lightning Source LLC
Chambersburg PA
CBHW042129100526
44587CB00026B/4223